THE WONDERS OF OUR WORLD

Oceans

Neil Morris

CRABTREE PUBLISHING COMPANY

www.crabtreebooks.com

The Wonders of our World

Crabtree Publishing Company

PMB 16A
350 Fifth Avenue
Suite 3308
New York, NY 10118

612 Welland Avenue
St. Catharines, Ontario
Canada L2M 5V6

73 Lime Walk
Headington
Oxford OX3 7AD
United Kingdom

Author: Neil Morris
Managing editor: Peter Sackett
Editors: Ting Morris & David Schimpky
Designer: Richard Rowan
Production manager: Graham Darlow
Picture research: Lis Sackett

Picture Credits:
Artists: Martin Camm.
Maps: European Map Graphics Ltd
Photographs: Bruce Coleman 11, Environmental Picture
Library 23 (bottom). Frank Lane 6, 7, 17 (bottom), 21 (top), 29.
G S F 12 (bottom). Caroline Jones 20 (top). Robert Harding
Picture library 14, 18 (top), 24 (top), 26 (top). Science Photo
Library 12 (top). Topham Picturepoint 3, 4, 5, 8, 10, I5, 16,
17 (top), 20 (bottom), 22, 23 (top), 24 (bottom), 25,
26 (bottom), 27, 28.

Cataloging-in-publication data

Morris, Neil
    Oceans

(Wonders of our world)
Includes index.
ISBN 0-86505-828-8 (library bound) ISBN 0-86505-840-7 (pbk.)
This book describes all aspects of oceans, including natural
features, ocean life, conservation, and shipping.

1. Oceans - Juvenile literature. 2. Marine biology - Juvenile
literature. I. Title. II. Series: Morris, Neil. Wonders of our
world.

GC21.5.M66 1995   j551.46   LC 95-31007

CONTENTS

WHAT IS AN OCEAN?

AN OCEAN is a huge body of salt water. There are five oceans around the world's continents—the Pacific, Atlantic, Indian, Arctic, and Southern oceans. The Southern, or Antarctic, Ocean surrounds the frozen continent of Antarctica and includes parts of three other oceans. The Pacific is the largest ocean.

Seas are smaller bodies of salt water and form parts of oceans. The biggest sea in the world, the South China Sea, is part of the Pacific Ocean.

OCEANS AND SEAS

It's easy to see that the Pacific is the largest ocean. It's nearly twice as big as the Atlantic and over 12 times bigger than the Arctic Ocean.

Seas are often almost completely surrounded by land and are connected to oceans by channels. Seas have other names too, such as Hudson Bay and the Gulf of Mexico.

Chukc Sea

Bering Strait

Gulf Alas

Pacific Ocean

TROPICAL WATERS

The Pacific Ocean stretches almost halfway around the earth. Small tropical islands dot this ocean. Here, the water is warm and inviting. Island coasts have lovely beaches, such as this one on Oahu, a Hawaiian island.

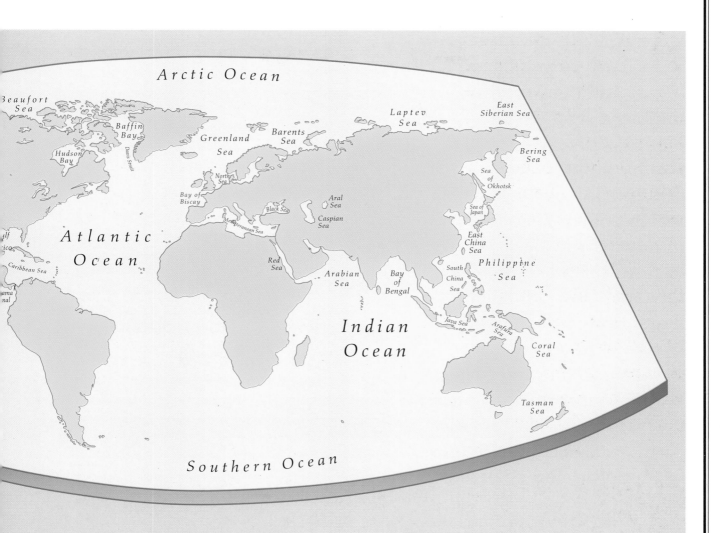

Arctic Ocean

Beaufort
Sea

Baffin
Bay

Greenland
Sea

Barents
Sea

Laptev
Sea

East
Siberian Sea

Hudson
Bay

Davis Strait

North
Sea

Bering
Sea

Bay of
Biscay

Black Sea

Aral
Sea

Caspian
Sea

Sea
of
Okhotsk

Sea of
Japan

Atlantic
Ocean

Mediteranean Sea

East
China
Sea

Caribbean Sea

Red
Sea

Arabian
Sea

Bay
of
Bengal

South
China
Sea

Philippine
Sea

Java Sea

Arafura
Sea

Indian
Ocean

Coral
Sea

Tasman
Sea

Southern Ocean

ABOVE THE ARCTIC CIRCLE

I N THE northern waters of the Atlantic and Arctic oceans, the sea is very cold. An Inuit hunter paddles his kayak past icebergs off the coast of Greenland.

WATERY PLANET

SCIENTISTS believe the earth formed from a cloud of gas and dust about 4.6 billion years ago. The young planet was very hot, and the surface was covered with volcanoes. They released steam, which cooled and condensed into water droplets. These fell back to earth as rain. The torrential rain collected into huge pools, which eventually became the oceans.

At first, one big, deep ocean covered most of the planet. Over millions of years the earth's oceans and continents have moved and changed.

EARLY, MOLTEN EARTH

This erupting volcano in Hawaii shows how the young planet Earth may have looked. At first the surface was probably so hot that rain turned back into steam as soon as it fell. At that time there was no life of any sort on the planet—no plants, animals, or people.

200 million years ago

180 million years ago

BLUE PLANET

This photograph of Earth was taken from an Apollo spacecraft. Our planet looks mainly blue and white from space. The blue is water, and the white is a layer of swirling clouds in the atmosphere. Here we can also see the brown and green land of Mexico and the southern United States. To the left is the vast Pacific Ocean, and in the middle is the narrow Gulf of California.

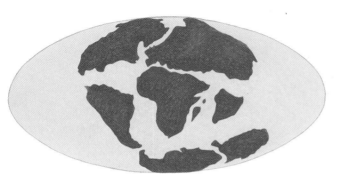

65 million years ago

MOVING CONTINENTS

ABOUT 200 million years ago, the earth's single huge continent began to split up into large pieces. As these pieces moved further apart, the Atlantic, Indian, Arctic, and Southern oceans were formed. The body of water that had surrounded the large continent became the Pacific Ocean.

MOVING WATER

THE OCEANS were first formed by rainfall, and today rainwater is constantly running into them through rivers. The amount of water in the oceans always stays about the same, however. It moves in a never-ending cycle.

Oceans affect our weather on land. Hurricanes are violent storms that often start at sea. Giant waves, called tsunamis, can cause great damage to coastal regions.

HOW THE CYCLE WORKS

HEAT FROM the sun evaporates water from the oceans, lakes, and green plants on land. The water vapor rises into the air, then cools to form tiny droplets. These join together to make clouds. When the droplets in the clouds get too heavy to float in the sky, they fall back to land as rain. Some rainwater soaks into the ground, but a great deal flows back to the ocean through rivers and streams. On the way, the water picks up minerals that make it salty. The water cycle then starts all over again.

OCEAN WAVES

WAVES are caused by wind blowing over water. They begin as tiny ripples, but by the time they reach the coast, they can be large and powerful. All over the world, people who live near coasts build defenses against high seas.

ENERGY FROM THE SEA

Wave energy can be used to make electricity. Some wave stations are out at sea, while others, like this one, are near the shore. As each wave hits the cliff, it forces water up the concrete tower. The water pushes air through a turbine, which turns an electric generator.

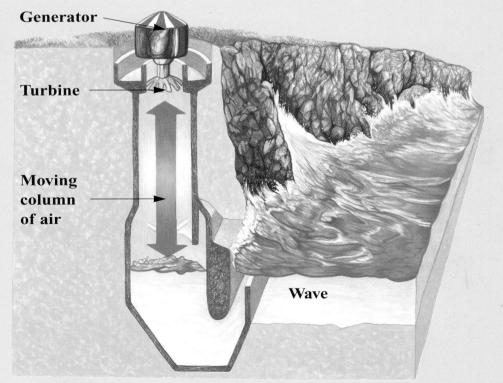

Generator

Turbine

Moving column of air

Wave

TIDES AND CURRENTS

OCEANS ARE never still. Twice a day, the water in oceans rises and then later goes down again. When water covers more land, we say that the tide has come in. The pull from the gravity of the moon and the sun causes tides.

The oceans also have currents, which are like rivers in the sea. Near the surface, currents are swept along by the wind. Deep-water currents are set in motion by differences in temperature and salinity—the amount of salt in the water.

COLD-CURRENT PENGUINS
Penguins like cold water, yet some live near the warm Galápagos Islands. This is because of a cold current which comes all the way from Antarctica.

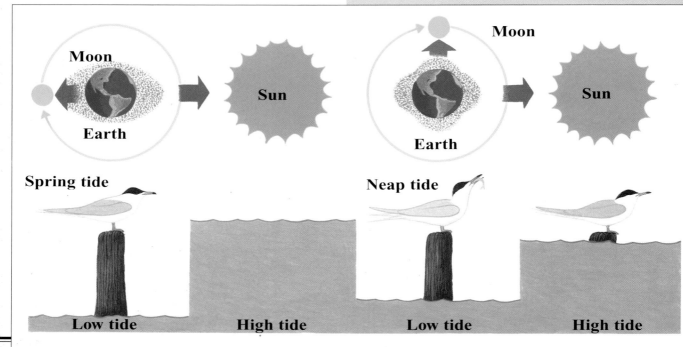

Moon
Sun
Earth

Moon
Sun
Earth

Spring tide

Neap tide

Low tide   High tide   Low tide   High tide

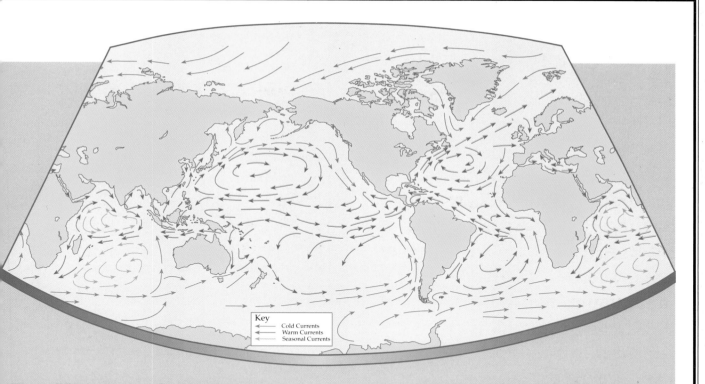

THE WORLD'S CURRENTS

The oceans are warmed in areas near the equator, the hottest part of the earth's surface. Currents help to spread this warmth across the globe.

Surface currents move in patterns that are roughly like circles. They move clockwise above the equator and counter-clockwise below it. The map shows the main warm and cold currents.

TIDAL RANGES

WHEN THE Sun, Moon, and Earth are in line (far left), the pull of gravity is greater, and there is a big difference between low and high tides. These are called spring tides, and they happen twice a month: at full moon and new moon. When the Sun and Moon are at right angles to the Earth (left), they produce smaller neap tides.

The Bay of Fundy (right), between the Canadian provinces of Nova Scotia and New Brunswick, has the world's biggest tides—14.5 meters (47 feet) between the high and low spring tides.

OCEAN FLOOR

THE EARTH'S outer layer, called its crust, is made up of huge pieces that fit together like a giant jigsaw puzzle. These pieces, called plates, are under the world's oceans and continents. Where the plates meet, they push against each other and buckle, making mountain ranges.

Plates buckle under the ocean, too. The ocean floor, like the continents, has mountains and valleys. Islands are actually mountaintops appearing above the sea.

DEEP-SEA EXPLORATION

At great depths, pressure would crumple ordinary submarines. Alvin, an American-built research vessel, has dived nearly 4 kilometers (2.5 miles) under the sea.

BLACK SMOKERS

SCIENTISTS aboard Alvin found stony chimneys on the ocean floor. They belch out hot, smoky water full of chemicals. Bacteria feed on these and provide food for crabs and worms.

NEW SEA BED

NEW crust is made when molten rock, called magma, breaks through ridges in the middle of the ocean floor. The new oceanic crust moves toward the continents. Volcanoes occur where oceanic crust is forced under continental crust.

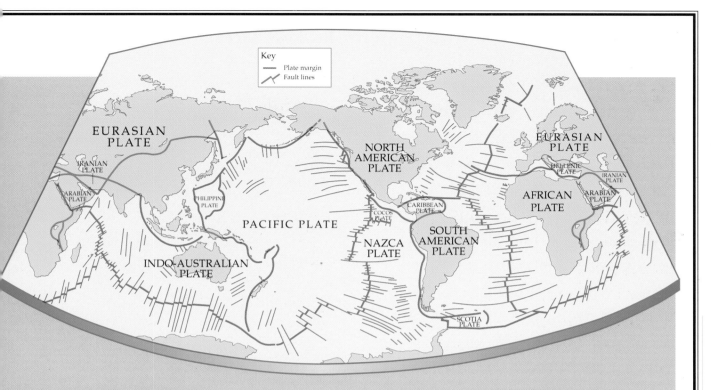

PLATES AND RIDGES

This map of the oceans shows where the world's spreading ridges are. The Mid-Atlantic Ridge forms the longest mountain range on earth.

The deepest part of the oceans is the Marianas Trench, in the Pacific Ocean. It is nearly 11 kilometers (7 miles) below sea level. Mount Everest is less than 9 kilometers (5.5 miles) above sea level.

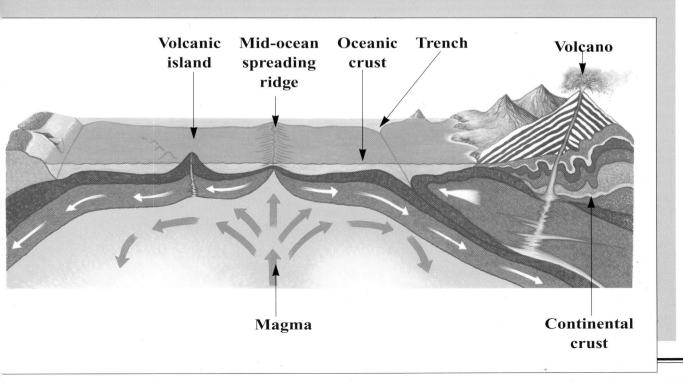

Volcanic island

Mid-ocean spreading ridge

Oceanic crust

Trench

Volcano

Magma

Continental crust

COASTLINES

WHERE THE ocean meets the land, there is often a battle between sea and rocks. As waves pound against the shore, they gradually wear away at the rocks. This process is called erosion.

Oceans carve the shapes of the world's coastlines. As waves batter high cliffs, rocks break off and fall to the shore. Wave action then smoothes these rocks into small round pebbles. Eventually, the pebbles are worn down into tiny fragments of sand, which collect on beaches.

The sand on beaches moves about as waves break on the shore. If you study a beach over time, you will see that it is always changing, especially after a storm.

WEARING AWAY

Cliffs of soft rock, such as chalk, are worn away more quickly than hard granite or basalt. Breakwaters and boulders can help protect the coast.

CORAL ISLANDS

The coasts of the tiny Maldive Islands, in the Indian Ocean, are protected by the coral reefs that surround them. Not one of the islands, however, is higher than 3 meters (10 feet). Any rise in sea level may threaten to submerge the islands.

FJORDS

GEIRANGER Fjord in Norway is a beautiful example of these long narrow inlets. Fjords lie between steep mountain slopes. They are actually the valleys of old glaciers that have been flooded by the sea, in this case, the Atlantic Ocean. The longest Norwegian fjord stretches over 200 kilometers (125 miles) inland. At its deepest point, it descends 1296 meters (4250 feet).

Coral islands are formed by the collection of debris from reefs. Corals look like plants, but they are really tiny animals related to jellyfish. A coral reef contains millions of these creatures, called polyps, which live together in colonies.

ICY WATERS

THE ARCTIC Ocean is completely frozen for most of the year. The permanent ice, called polar ice, can be up to 50 meters (165 feet) thick in winter, but it melts to about 2 meters (6.5 feet) in summer. The North Pole lies in the middle of this sea ice.

The South Pole is on Antarctica. The Southern Ocean surrounds this frozen continent. In winter, much of this ocean is covered with ice.

PACK ICE

THE EDGES of thick polar ice are surrounded by blocks of floating, frozen sea water. These blocks are called pack ice, and they can be up to 2 meters (6.5 feet) thick. Chunks of pack ice are broken up and then pushed together again by the movement of the ocean. The ice is constantly changing and can make fantastic shapes. Pack ice forms a huge drifting ice belt around Antarctica, making it difficult to reach the frozen continent by ship in winter. In the summer, however, icebreakers can cut through.

ICEBERGS

BOTH polar regions are littered with icebergs. These floating islands of ice have broken away from glaciers and ice shelves. This iceberg is in Baffin Bay, off Greenland. Only the tip of an iceberg shows above sea level.

PANCAKE ICE

When sea water freezes, it first forms thin, round slabs of ice. These slabs may be up to 3 meters (10 feet) across. Because of the way they look, the slabs are called pancake ice. They jostle together and, as the temperature continues to drop, they get harder and thicker. Slowly, a sheet of ice forms from the slabs.

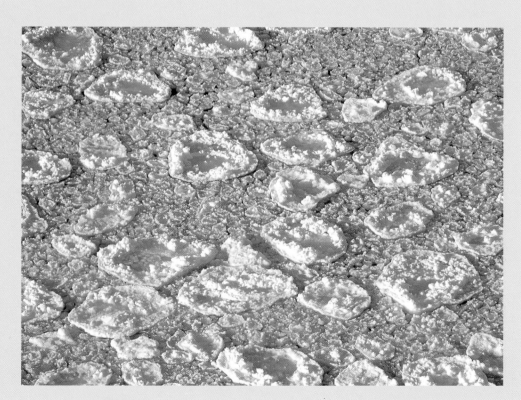

OCEAN LIFE

MILLIONS OF creatures live in the sea. Many swim near the surface; others live at the bottom of the ocean. The smallest are plankton, tiny plants and animals that get their energy from sunlight. Blue whales, which can weigh over 150,000 kilograms (330,000 pounds), are the largest of all.

All ocean creatures are linked together by what they eat. This food chain starts with plankton, which are eaten by small fish, which are in turn eaten by larger fish. It ends with sharks and whales, which are hunted only by humans.

GREAT BARRIER REEF
Over 1500 species of fish live in the warm waters of the Great Barrier Reef (above), off the coast of Australia. Sharks feed in deeper waters nearby.

IN THE DEPTHS

THE angler fish lives in the cold, dark depths. It has a special fin over its mouth, which glows with light. The light attracts small fish into the angler's wide-open jaws.

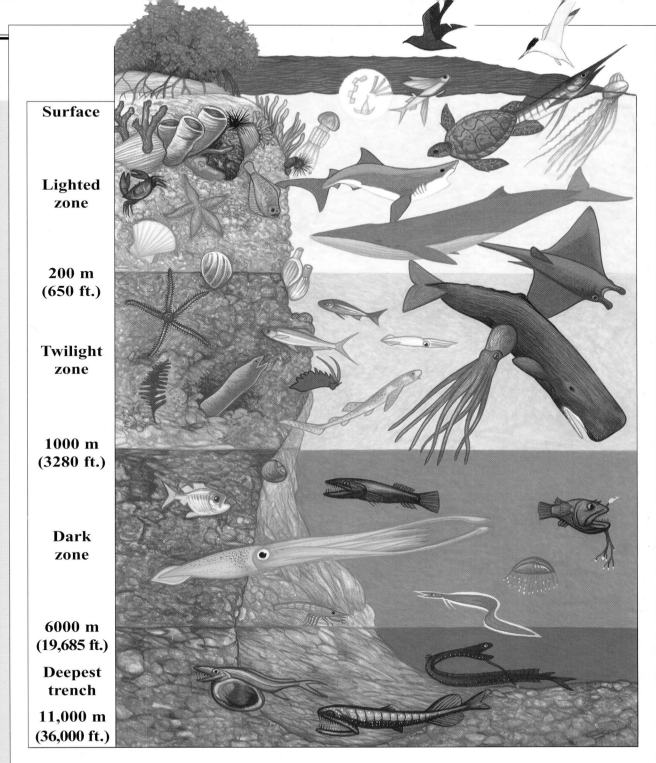

Surface

Lighted
zone

200 m
(650 ft.)

Twilight
zone

1000 m
(3280 ft.)

Dark
zone

6000 m
(19,685 ft.)

Deepest
trench

11,000 m
(36,000 ft.)

DEPTH ZONES

MOST SEA plants live in the top 150 meters (492 feet) of the ocean, where light penetrates the water. This region is crowded with sea life.

Farther down is a twilight zone. Below about 1000 meters (3280 feet), the ocean is completely dark all the time and there is no plant life. When plankton die, they sink, providing food for the deep-sea dwellers.

LIFE ON THE SEASHORE

THE SEASHORE is teeming with animals and plants that depend on the daily tides. Some live on the flat, sandy areas exposed at low tide. Sandworms and razor clams bury themselves in the sand until the water returns. On rocky shores, shellfish hide in their shells until the tide rolls in. Small fish are often left stranded in rocky tidal pools. At high tide, the flooded seashore comes alive again.

SEAWEED

Seaweeds belong to a group of plants called algae. They often live in tidal pools and shallow coastal waters. Seaweeds have rootlike organs called holdfasts, which cling to rocks. Most seaweeds are tough and rubbery, so they can survive ocean storms as well as the time they spend out of water.

CRABS

LIVING around tidal pools, crabs often hide under rocks or seaweed. They eat small animals and the remains of dead creatures. Crabs have strong pincers for grasping food and sharp mouthparts for crunching shellfish.

PUFFINS

THESE sea birds live in large groups on cliffs high above the seashore. Puffins dive into the sea and use their wings to swim underwater. They catch small fish in their large colorful beaks.

USING SPACE

Animals and plants compete with each other for space on the seashore. The lower shore is covered by sea most of the time and is full of life. The middle shore is exposed to the air twice a day for a few hours and is home to sea anemones and limpets. Barnacles and snails called periwinkles live on the upper shore, which is rarely covered by sea. Some creatures, such as the small periwinkle, have adapted to life in the splash zone.

Splash zone

Upper shore

Middle shore

Lower shore

FOOD FROM THE SEA

PEOPLE HAVE always caught fish and other sea creatures for food. In the past, fishing boats were small and did not sail far from their home port. Fishers caught seafood for local people.

Today we use big ships, vast deep-sea nets, and sonar devices to trap huge quantities of fish. Overfishing is a big problem for some species of fish and fishing grounds. International agreements say where and how much people can fish, but these often end in disputes.

FISHING INDUSTRY
Small trawlers like this one find it very difficult to compete with larger ships. Many boats are run by family businesses that are now struggling.

DEEP-SEA SHIPS

BIG deep-sea trawlers and factory ships can travel long distances and haul huge catches of fish on board. The fish are cleaned and stored in a refrigerated hold to keep them fresh until the ship returns to port.

SEAFOOD

FISH and shellfish are nutritious foods. At this restaurant in Spain, customers look at the fresh seafood before deciding what they would like to order.

Fish is popular in Spain, but the country with the biggest fishing catch is Japan. In Japan, fish are cooked in a variety of ways. Raw fish called *sushi* is a favorite dish.

WHALING

Many kinds of whales have been hunted to the point where they are nearly extinct. Despite an international ban, some countries still hunt these sea mammals. Many people are concerned about the survival of whales. By protesting, they hope to put an end to whaling.

MINERALS

THE SEA bed contains minerals in the same way that land does. Minerals float in sea water or lie on the sea floor. These minerals, however, are often difficult and expensive to collect.

Undersea oil, however, is easier to extract. The first undersea oil was found off the coast of California in 1891. Today, about one-fifth of the world's oil and natural gas comes from under the sea. There are oil rigs in oceans and seas around the globe.

SEA SALT
In hot coastal countries, salt is extracted from the ocean by leaving sea water in large, shallow pans. The water is slowly evaporated by the heat of the sun, leaving salt behind.

DREDGING
Sand, gravel, and other minerals can be scooped up from the sea bed by special ships called dredgers. In the Pacific, small black lumps containing nickel, manganese, copper, cobalt, and iron are dredged from the deep ocean floor.

OIL RIG

A N OIL RIG has a fixed platform with drilling machinery and living quarters for workers. The platform with a big H is a helipad, where a helicopter can land. Workers arrive by helicopter.

The platform is built on land and towed out to sea, where it rests on a frame of steel supports. These extend down to the sea bed, where they are bolted in place. After drilling, the oil or gas is carried along pipelines to tankers or to a refinery on shore.

CROSSING THE OCEANS

THE FIRST ocean travelers probably paddled along in dugout canoes. The ancient Egyptians invented sails about 5000 years ago. Wind powered most ships until the mid-1800s, when steam engines and propellers were developed. Most large ocean-going ships are now powered by diesel engines.

Today, most people cross oceans by airplane because it is faster than traveling by ship. Luxury liners, however, are still popular for holiday cruises. Ferries carry passengers on shorter trips. Most cargo is still carried by ships, since it is less costly than transporting cargo by plane.

SEA-GOING CANOES
Traditionally, the people of the Solomon Islands, in the Pacific Ocean, go to sea in huge wooden dug-outs. Their canoes can carry up to 100 people.

SUBMARINES
Nuclear-powered submarines can travel beneath the ocean for months without surfacing. Their propeller is driven by steam made by a nuclear engine.

LINKING OCEANS

THE Panama Canal crosses Central America to link the Atlantic and Pacific oceans. It is 81 kilometers (50 miles) long. Ships cross the canal through a series of locks. Locks are enclosures that fill with water to raise a ship to the next level.

SUPERTANKER

Giant supertankers carry crude oil around the world, much of it from the oil-rich countries of the Middle East. The largest tanker is over 485 meters (1600 feet) long.

The largest group of supertankers, called ultralarge crude carriers, or ULCCs, can carry 500 million kilograms (over 1 billion pounds) of oil. They are much too big to dock in most harbors.

SAVING OUR SEAS

FOR MANY years people have been using the ocean as an easy place to dump their garbage. Industrial pollution and sewage are poisoning the world's oceans. Many people are now aware of this problem, and are working to fix it.

Governments and scientists all around the world must cooperate to ensure that no more damage is done. People need to take more care when using the oceans.

GARBAGE DUMP

SOME PEOPLE use seashores as garbage dumps. Others dispose of waste by putting it directly into the ocean. Although all pollution harms the oceans, waste put in the water is very dangerous because it is hard to spot and correct.

OIL SPILLS

MOST OIL spills are accidental, but during the Persian Gulf War in 1991 over 800 million kilograms (1.7 billion pounds) of oil were deliberately released into the gulf. The oil quickly spread over the coastline. This cormorant (left) was just one of the birds affected.

Small boats with powerful lights helped to clean up a huge oil spill from a supertanker in 1989 (right). Over 1700 kilometers (1056 miles) of Alaskan coastline were polluted by oil.

NATIONAL PARKS

One way to conserve our oceans and coasts is to have more protected areas. Australia's Great Barrier Reef, including tiny Heron Island (right), is a vast marine park. In Florida, Biscayne National Park is made up of islands, reefs, and coastal waters.

GLOSSARY

Atmosphere   The layer of air and other gases surrounding the earth.

Bacteria   Tiny one-celled organisms.

Breakwater   A barrier built out in the sea to break up the force of waves.

Channel   A narrow stretch of water connecting oceans and seas.

Conservation   Preserving the environment and the world's natural resources.

Continent   One of the earth's seven huge land masses.

Coral   A tiny animal, called a polyp, that forms colonies in warm, shallow waters.

Crust   The hard outer layer of the earth.

Current   A strong, steady flow of water in one direction.

Dredge   To remove material from the sea floor.

Equator   An imaginary circle that stretches around the middle of the earth.

Erosion   The wearing away of rocks by the action of water and wind.

Evaporate   To change from a liquid to a vapor.

Fjord   A long narrow inlet of the sea between high cliffs.

Generator   A device that makes electricity.

Glacier   A slowly moving mass of ice.

Gravity   The force that pulls things toward the center of a star or planet.

Holdfast   The organ by which seaweeds cling to rocks.

Hurricane   A severe, destructive tropical storm.

Iceberg	A large mass of ice floating in the sea.
Ice shelf	A mass of ice floating on the sea, yet attached to land.
Kayak	A canoe-like boat with a light covered frame.
Magma	Hot molten rock beneath the earth's surface.
Mineral	A substance that occurs naturally in the earth.
Molten	Melted; turned into liquid.
Pack ice	Blocks of floating, frozen sea water.
Plankton	Tiny drifting plants and animals that live near the surface of the sea.
Plate	A huge piece of the earth's crust.
Pollution	Poisonous and harmful substances that damage natural environments.
Salinity	Saltiness (of water).
Sewage	Human waste matter.
Sonar	A position-finding device used in the water.
Tide	The rise and fall of sea level.
Tropics	The areas around the equator; the hottest part of the earth's surface.
Tsunami	A giant wave caused by a volcanic eruption or an earthquake.
Turbine	A machine with a turning blade.
Volcano	An opening where molten rock and gas come from deep inside the earth.
Whaling	Hunting and killing whales.

INDEX

A
Alvin research vessel 12
angler fish 18
Antarctic Ocean *see* Southern Ocean
Arctic Ocean 4, 5, 7, 16
Atlantic Ocean 4, 5, 7, 15, 27

B
Baffin Bay 16
Bay of Fundy 11
Biscayne National Park 29

C
canoes 26
cargo ships 26
coastlines 4, 14-15, 20, 21, 29
conservation 28-29
continental crust 12, 13
continents 6, 7, 12
coral 14-15, 29
crabs 20
currents 10-11

D
deep-sea exploration 12
deep-sea ships 22
depth zones 19
dredgers 24

E
energy 9, 18
erosion 14

F
fishing 22-23
fjords 15
food chain 18

G
Galápagos Islands 10
Great Barrier Reef 18, 29

H
hurricanes 8

I
ice 16-17
Indian Ocean 4, 7, 14
islands 4, 14-15, 29

L
luxury liners 26

M
magma 12, 13
Maldive Islands 14
Mid-Atlantic Ridge 13
minerals 24

N
national parks 29

O
ocean floor 12-13
ocean life 14, 15, 18-19, 20, 21, 22, 23
oceanic crust 12, 13
oceans, formation of 6-7
oil 24, 25, 28, 29
oil rigs 24-25
oil spills 29

P
Pacific Ocean 4, 7, 13, 24, 26, 27
Panama Canal 27
penguins 10
Persian Gulf 29
plankton 18, 19
plates 12, 13
pollution 28-29
puffins 21

R
ridges 13

S
sea birds 21
sea salt 24
seafood 22-23
seashore zones 21
seaweed 20
Southern Ocean 4, 7, 16-17
submarines 26
supertanker 27

T
tidal pools 20-21
tides 10-11
trenches 13
tsunamis 8

V
volcanoes 6, 12

W
water cycle 8-9
waves 8, 9, 14
whales 18, 23

56789 Printed in the U.S.A. 43